MEDICINE for *Healing*

By Robin McCray

MEDICINE FOR HEALING
The Word of God
Robin McCray

Published by Pecan Tree Publishing,
June 2011
www.pecantreepress.com

Various scriptural references noted throughout

Library of Congress Control Number: 2011931140
ISBN: 978-0-9832078-8-7

PECAN TREE PUBLISHING

Hollywood, Fl.

www.pecantreepress.com

New Voices | New Styles | New Vision

Table of Contents

Dedication/Acknowledgments

First and foremost, I thank my Lord and Savior Jesus Christ for calling me for such a time as this to administer His Word to many. I dedicate this book in the memory of my father-in-law, George W. McCray, Sr. I'll never forget the godly wisdom he deposited into my life. He shared many profound words that helped me to reach this point in my life. I'll never forget his words: "Do not abort your purpose, there's greatness and hidden treasures inside of you that comes from God."

It seems that I have labored over this book for several years. Believe it or not I wrote this book in a week. There was so much inside of me for a long time. It started flowing out for such a time as this. This is one of many books I've written. I've carried the messages of this book within me for a period of time. Now I have given birth!

I want to thank my husband, my friend and partner for life, Troy. Thank you for helping me to unfold who God called me to be in Him and encouraging me all the way. Thanks to my children, Jasmine, Troy II and Jerami and other family members for your many endeavors. You all were my greatest support and strength. Thanks to my mother; Earthline Smith and mother-in-law; Beatrice McCray, my sister Mary Stewart and the entire Faircloth and McCray family. You all have been such a source of strength and blessing in many times of need.

I want to take a moment to acknowledge some great leaders and spiritual covering the Lord placed in my life. Thanks to my mentors, Pastor Mae McCray Brooks (In loving memory), Bishop Harold Calvin Ray and Pastor Brenda Ray of Redemptive Life Fellowship, Pastors John and Ericka McCrutcheon of Joint Heirs Fellowship Church (Houston, TX), Pastors Bobby and Annette Gilbert of In the Word Praise and Worship Center in West Palm Beach, FL. Thank you all for your wisdom and spiritual guidance for equipping and teaching me over the years. Thanks to all the ladies in covenant with "Sisters on the Wall." Thank you all for affecting my life beyond measure.

I also want to also acknowledge those who have made an impact on me through my journey; those who have served as mentors over the years: Pastors Benjamin and Kathleen Hawkins, (my intercessory partners); and special thanks to Renette Manual, Prophetess Torrie Mack, First Lady Katrina Grainger, Rhonda Lynn Scott, and Marcia Mitchell for your friendship and support. Thank you all for your prayers and spirit of encouragement.

Lastly, I wish my professor Dr. Crow (a Southern Baptist) of Barry University was alive to witness this book. But I believe he is looking down from heaven and smiling. He saw the hidden well of gifts inside me. As a student he helped me to see the diamond in the rough and aided by pulling out the creative ways of writing to the surface. He also trained me how to give presentations and speak with a spirit of boldness (confidence) in front of an audience.

I am deeply indebted to each of you. Thank you, Lord, for the privilege of sharing your Word to many.

MEDICINE FOR HEALING
THE WORD OF GOD

"My Son, attend to my words; incline thine ear unto my sayings. Let them not depart from thine eyes; keep them in the midst of thine heart. For they are life unto those that find them, and health to all their flesh—Proverbs 4:20-22

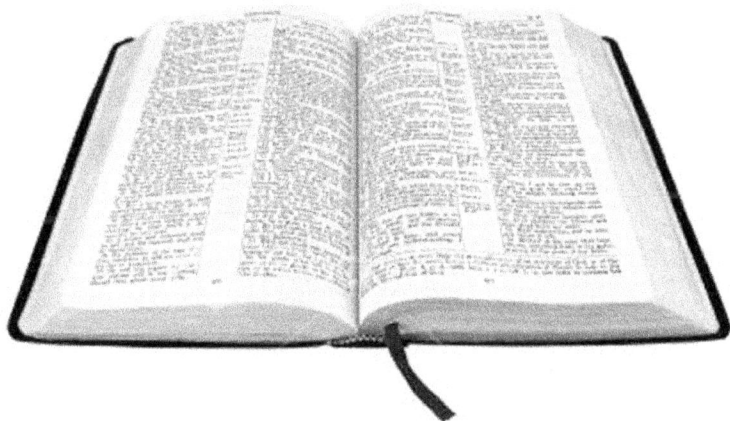

Introduction

The purpose of the book is to bring healing to many who are stricken with all forms of sickness, disease and infirmities. In February 2005, my body was attacked with an illness. I experienced heart palpitations, anxiety attacks, and pain in my breast area. Later in the same year my body was attacked by cancer, which moved to my joints causing a lot of pain. I would only sleep two to three hours each night because of the pain; that lasted for six months. During this time, I died spiritually. I stopped reading the Word of God and fellowshipping with the God of the Word. But the Spirit of the Lord sure has a plan of restoration; and a way of turning you back to the original intent your purpose on earth—His purpose! Only God knows what it takes to bring an individual back. He is after all married to the back slider and knows what it takes to restore their love and joy.

I thought my life was over! God had a plan and purpose for my life {Jeremiah 29:11}. I had to walk through a process. As I repented for being out of fellowship with Him, the Spirit of the Lord begin to take me step-by-step (a process) towards total healing. During those nights when I did not sleep, He walked me through His Word and revealed or awakened me to His healing scriptures. He told me to "SPEAK" His Word into my life. I believe many Believers are not healed because they do not know what they already have. See, the devil wants to keep us in the dark (in ignorance) about the things of the Kingdom.

I remember growing up and hearing people say things like: What you do not know will not hurt you. But when I came to know the Lord, I found out that what you do not know will not only hurt you, but it will destroy you. The Word of God tells us in Hosea 4:6 "My people [Believers] are destroyed for lack of knowledge." We perish and stay in the dark from what we do not know...the knowledge [light]...the things that are freely given to us. NOT knowing the great truths contained in the Word of God is dangerous and defeating; surely we can conclude that ignorance of Jehovah's Will can bring nothing but tragedy to the Body of Christ.

The Word of God tells us in 1 Peter 2:9b "...who hath called you out of darkness [ignorance] into His marvelous light [knowledge]." According to Psalm 103, verse 2, we have benefits given to use when we accept the Lord as Savior. Healing is one of the benefits of the Kingdom of God.

I've learned through my experience that sometimes healing is a process. There are two kinds of faith: The first one is "Delivering Faith." This is when God "instantly" turns your situation around. The second one is "Sustaining Faith." This takes a greater faith and a deeper walk with God. This is when circumstances do not change immediately, but you say: "God, I do not care what comes against me. I do not care how long it takes; this thing is not going to get me down. I know you are on my side. As long as you are for me, that's all that matters. Sustaining Faith is what gets you through those dark nights of the soul, when you do not know where to go or what to do, and it seems that you cannot last another day. But because of your faith in God, you do. Over the next few pages, I am honored to take you on my journey to total wholeness for the body. I hope my testimony encourages you on your journey.

My experience was the second kind of faith; "sustaining faith." Each day, as the pain in my joints grew worse, I descended to a point in my life where I was desperate for help. I became like the woman with the issue of blood recorded in Matthew chapter nine of the Bible. One day, by the leading of the Holy Spirit, I was led to read Proverbs 4:20-22.

Because of my Christian walk and knowledge of the Word, I knew I was already healed. The Word of Gods says I am. Therefore, I knew I was under a spiritual attack and it was time for me to get serious and go into warfare.

The first thing that I got into my spirit was 1 Peter 2:24 that states; "Who Himself bore our sins in His own body on the tree, that we, having died to sins, might live for righteousness — by whose stripes you were healed."

This scripture reminded me that my healing was in the past tense; signifying that it is has already been accomplished! The Spirit of the Lord revealed to me that it only takes "one" scripture to believe, receive and act upon for His glory (my healing) to manifest.

I could not understand why my body was not healed immediately like some of the scriptures recorded. There are numerous recounts of people being healed immediately as Jesus touched them; they were made whole promptly. The Holy Spirit revealed that in some cases healing is a process and therefore it will not come instantly. So, I began to meditate and focus on healing scriptures such as:

Isaiah 53:4-5 - "Surely He has borne our griefs and carried our sorrows; yet we esteemed Him stricken, smitten by God, and afflicted. 5 But He was wounded for our transgressions, He was bruised for our iniquities; the chastisement for our peace was upon Him, and by His stripes we are healed."

Galatians 3:13-14 - "Christ has redeemed us from the curse of the law, having become a curse for us (for it is written, "Cursed is everyone who hangs on a tree"), 14 that the blessing of Abraham might come upon the Gentiles in Christ Jesus, that we might receive the promise of the Spirit through faith."

Mark 11:23-24 - "For assuredly, I say to you, whoever says to this mountain, 'Be removed and be cast into the sea,' and does not doubt in his heart, but believes that those things he says will be done, he will have whatever he says. 24 Therefore I say to you, whatever things you ask when you pray, believe that you receive them, and you will have them."

Psalm 107:20 - "He sent His word and healed them, and delivered them from their destructions."

Exodus 15:26 - "If you diligently heed the voice of the Lord your God and do what is right in His sight, give ear to His commandments and keep all His statutes, I will put none of the diseases on you which I have brought on the Egyptians. For I am the Lord who heals you."

Proverbs 4:20-23 - "My son, give attention to my words; incline your ear to my sayings. 21 Do not let them depart from your eyes; keep them in the midst of your heart; 22 For they are life to those who find them, and health to all their flesh. 23 Keep your heart with all diligence, for out of it spring the issues of life."

In Romans 10:17 the Word tells us that—"Faith comes by hearing and hearing the Word of God." I took the Word literally and began to quote these scriptures out loud every day, sometimes 3-5 times daily. It was just like taking the recommended dosage of medicine, but instead, I took the Word of God. I made a conscious decision; I made up my mind and made a commitment based on Psalm 118:17, that I shall live and not die and declare the works of the Lord. Every day on my lunch break, instead of running errands, I would sit in my car and get quiet and listen to the Lord and let Him minister and encourage me.

Each day I would study and meditate and SPEAK the Word until the Word became a part of me. Like it says in John 1:14…the word became flesh—the Word became a reality to me. I took a strong stand of authority and commanded the spirit of infirmity that was in my body to leave in Jesus' Name and declared that it had no legal right to be there. I began to lay hold of the promises of God's Word. He said that His Word will never return to Him void (Isaiah 55:11) AND that He's active and alert watching over his Word to perform it (Jeremiah 1:12).

His Word was returned to Him when I took hold of it personally and spoke it out. One thing that kept me going was the Scripture found in Jeremiah 23:29 that says the Word of God is like a fire and a like a hammer that breaks the rock in pieces. Even though the problem seemed to get worse, I stayed with God's promises, knowing the Word was breaking the sickness in my body into pieces. January 23, 2007 I remember writing these words on my calendar, "MY DIVINE HEALING MANI-FESTED!" I took communion; and praise God, my healing manifested that day.

As you can see my healing did not come immediately. I had to first, take God at His Word then believe, receive and act on it. That was my process and I am thankful for it. Let's get started building your faith so that you too may receive your healing. Amen.

Jesus,

Open my ears to hear your words clearly. I hunger to feed on heavenly manna, which is truth and life for me.

Amen.

CHAPTER 1

Words of Life

The first scripture the Spirit of Lord led me to was Proverbs 4:20-22; *"My son, attend to my words, incline thine ear unto my sayings. Let them not depart from thine eyes; keep them in the midst of thine heart. For they are life unto those that find them, and health to all their flesh."*

When we become born again, we receive the eternal life of God. Eternity has no beginning and no ending, and even death has no hold on us. There is no death to a born-again believer (Galatians 2:20). We have already died the only death required of us. The only difference physical death makes to the born-again believer is the transfer of the life of God from earth to heaven. We do not have to wait until we get to heaven to become healthy, wealthy, and wise. A victorious life is available to us on earth now.

Solomon told his son in Proverbs to pay attention to his words, because they are life--not that they are going to be or hope to be or may be in heaven--but they are life and health for you today.

The Word "brings life" and "health to all their flesh." I started to get excited. Something was happening within me. My spirit man began to leap! My faith began to rise up. The Word of God tells us in **John 6:63**; "....the words that I speak unto you, they are *spirit* and they are *life.*

The Spirit of the Lord revealed that I needed to arise and sharpen the "spiritual" weapons that were already made available to me through the blood of Jesus and by the authority of His name. If you are ready to get some ammunition this book is loaded with bullets of revelation that will knock out the enemy and bring wholeness to your body. But before we load and shoot, we must take a moment to clean out the barrel—to make sure we know what we are doing.

God's Holy Scriptures are indeed infallible. The Word is incapable of making mistakes or being wrong. The inspired Word of God never fails and is always effective. One of the missing ingredients in experiencing the Word of God is *praying the Word back to God.* **Prayer** is the force that revitalizes and activates God's Word, with resulting answers—something happens—helping to birth and bring forth God's purposes on earth. Almighty God has already sent forth His Word, and when we take it by faith and lay claim to it in our hearts and give it voice we are *establishing* His Word in the earth.

The Lord *hears* us when we *pray according to His Word* which is His will [1 John 5:14-15], so when praying The Word over ourselves or our loved ones we only need to ask once if we ask in faith from the heart. Prayer works; especially when it is based on the Word of God. I love what Isaiah 55:11 says, *"So shall My Word be that goes forth from my mouth; it shall not return to Me void; but it shall accomplish what I please, and it shall prosper in the thing for which I sent it."* God's Word is returned when we give voice to it!

The Bible has much to say about the important role our words play in our lives, especially when we are speaking the Word of God over our situations. No, it is not mind over matter—it is God's Word over the matter. We need to learn not to focus on the problems but to focus on the answer. *Continually* speaking and laying claim to the Word of God will bring about the desired change.

Everything God does will be based on His Word. The words that we speak are seeds that go into an incubator. The key is—continuing to speak faith-filled words over your circumstance no matter what it looks like; until it manifests.

I believe as we *proclaim* or *speak* or *prophesy* or *reveal* the Word of God, which is the will of God, to an adverse, out of order situation, there is always an action, there is always a noise. You cannot reveal Jesus, who is the way, the truth and the life to a dry or lifeless situation without it being affected. You may not hear it, but be assured there **IS** an action and there **IS** a noise. Something will always happen. The Word of God **IS** life and brings life. This action always begins in the spirit and if we will refuse to give up or change our belief and confession, our miracle of life will eventually begin to materialize within our natural situation.

The prophetic voice shatters the enemy. We must prophesy and declare God's purposes, speaking to the valley of dry bones. Know that what God has promised in His Word for you is also His will for your situation. As believers, we have to speak to those mountains or obstacles and stand firm in our confession believing the Word of God and watch God move on our behalf.

Sweet Holy Spirit,

Show me in your word and reveal in my spirit what I already have for my healing—in Jesus' name.

Amen

FROM THIS CHAPTER, I BELIEVE GOD'S PRESCRIPTION FOR ME IS:

_____

_____

_____

_____

_____

_____

_____

_____

_____

_____

_____

_____

CHAPTER 2

What Do You Have?

Picture in your mind a man throwing a ball to another man. The man on the receiving end catches it and has a *firm hold on it* as he draws it close to his body.

Did you see that? He *caught it* and had *possession of it*. Now what do you have?

The "ball" represents the promises of God.

Faith is being sure, holding on to, and holding true to what is true, to the Word the God has given us. For His word is faithful and true.

God has given us the promise, it is sure, it is true and it is established. We must stand in faith until the manifestation, and then we must by faith and action **possess** the promise.

Possession: something seized, an *acquisition, to have and to hold*

Seize: to possess or take by force, to take hold of, to attack or overwhelm physically.

Many times we find ourselves believing, even being in faith but we stop short of possessing. To possess is to take, seize, take hold of, hold on to – make your own – So much a part of us that nothing can remove, alter, take away, decrease, modify, dilute etc. the promise of God. Circumstances do not change the word of God, The word of God change circumstances! If it's mine then I have it. I POSSESS it.

Like the woman with the issue of blood, we must determine to press past the barriers and obstacles that stand between God's provision and us. Right now at this moment you can take ownership (possession) of your healing.

Say out loud: **"I have the blessing of the Lord; I have what the Word of God says I can have. I have health and I have all that Jesus purchased for me to have. I take it by faith and I lay claim to it now."**

Yes, receive your healing by faith! Real Bible faith is faith in the love of God. In order to believe God's Word, we must first believe He loves us. When we believe the love God has for us, we know we have a *right* to forgiveness, answered prayers, healing, deliverance, and more. Faith is not an abstract idea or concept; it is a practical expression of your confidence in God and His Word. Faith is substance that *activates* the promises of

God in your life. If you want to see results in the Kingdom of God, you must have faith!

As Christians we are entitled to everything that Jesus bought and paid for with His Blood (the entire Word of God). Look beyond your circumstances to the promises contained in the Word, see yourself enjoying them, know they are a reality and will be manifesting soon. Do not complain to the Lord about your situation. Do not grow complacent and learn to live with the problem. Get busy standing on the Word and get rid of the problem. Take a proactive stand of rejecting it completely through the Word.

When I was going through the process of waiting for total wholeness in my body, instead of going out to lunch, I would take long walks (everyday), reading the scriptures pertaining to healing, claiming them over my body, rebuking that sickness/disease, and commanding it to leave in Jesus' name.

Check yourself out before the Lord for any un-forgiveness or any "open doors" you may have to the enemy—repent and make changes as quickly as possible. Do not forget about your provision in 1 John 1:9: "that if we confess our sins, He is faithful and just to forgive us our sins and to cleanse us from all unrighteousness." Remember sin will block the blessings of God. *So get rid of all of the blessing blockers!*

Some healings are instant and some take a few hours or even months before the healing is complete. If you are **waiting for your healing** keep thanking Jesus.

Lay your hands on yourself and **command** the sickness to leave, **command** your body to line up with the **Word of God.**

Daily, I would read out loud the healing scriptures, inserting my name in them where applicable, making them personal. You can also use the name of others that you are praying for in those Scriptures. I would actively meditate, ponder, and chew on the truth of these Scriptures. Remember the Word of God is His personal love letter to you. I would do this three times a day or more until my faith was built up for healing, then once a day to maintain my faith. Romans 10:17 says that *faith comes by hearing and hearing by the Word of God.* Build your faith and your doubts will starve to death! Amen.

It is of utmost importance that you make God's Word the final authority in your life. You must become convinced in your heart, knowing clearly from the Scriptures, that healing is a purchased possession for you. Make up your mind that you will not settle for anything less than what He promised for your life through His Word.

I encourage you to take a firm, proactive approach and go after it, knowing the right of health was bought and paid, and a wonderful gift that Jesus gave to the Church by His redemptive act on the Cross. When any type of sickness or disease tries to come upon you, IMMEDIATELY speak it out with a certainty, knowing what belongs to you.

SPEAK OUT: *"I do not have sickness (disease or pain), what I have is the Word of God and all the blessings associated with it. I am healed of the Lord, I am not sick!"* Then command the problem to leave in the name of Jesus Christ! And do it over and over, every time it comes to mind, until it leaves and healing is manifested in your body.

FATHER,
In the name of your son Jesus,
I speak to my faith and I com-
mand it rise up! I believe it is
done.

Amen

FROM THIS CHAPTER, I BELIEVE GOD'S PRESCRIPTION FOR ME IS:

_____

_____

_____

_____

_____

_____

_____

_____

_____

_____

_____

_____

CHAPTER 3

Build your Faith Up

In the Book of Jude, Jesus' brother Jude motivates us with an action plan to keep ourselves in God's love through three actions.

Jude verse 20; *"But ye, beloved, building up yourselves on your most holy faith, praying in the Holy Ghost."*

First, we are to build ourselves up in our faith. Building ourselves up in our faith involves growing in our knowledge of the truth. Building takes effort. You need a building plan, resources, a team of co-builders, and time available for the building. Studying the Word, soaking up its truths, and then applying that truth in our lives builds us up in our faith.

Second, we are to pray in the power of the Holy Spirit. By praying passionately and wholeheartedly we discern the mind of God. We communicate with God, listen to Him, and then obey Him. Sometimes we fall into doing only one or two of these steps, but possibly not the other one or two. It is literally life changing when we communicate with God, listen to what He has to say about His will for our lives and then obey. This is enjoying the presence of God!

Praying is an activity that has eternal significance. God's kingdom is advanced when we pray as His will is done. Matthew 6:10, "your kingdom come, your will be done on earth as it is in heaven."

Finally, we are to eagerly await the coming of our Lord Jesus Christ. Longing for eternal life reveals that the center of our existence is not this world, but the next one. We live in this world, but are not of this world.

We must exert effort and diligence to keep ourselves in God's love, but finally and ultimately we are victorious because of the grace of God. Behind all of this effort is His sustaining grace. He is the one who prevents us from falling.

Praying is central to building up our faith and keeping ourselves in God's love as we eagerly wait for the return of Jesus.

Acts 14:8-10 *"The lame man, who has never walked in his entire life is able to walk after "exercising faith" in the power of God."*

The man in this passage "heard" Paul speaking. Paul is preaching the power of God in Lystra. He speaks a word of faith that stirs something within the man that he has never felt before. He hears a word that supernaturally attacks his disability, a word that is greater than his condition. This gets his full attention—the transforming power of God begins to fight what the man hasn't felt his entire life. The word you receive is a critical element in the fulfillment of your purpose. The Word of God *attacks, uproots* and *destroys* the foundations of the negative issues in your life.

Secondly, Paul observes the man intently and sees that he has the faith to be healed (v.9). Notice that the Scripture does not gloss over the man's condition. Faith will *connect* you to your deliverance. When the lame man "hears" of the power of God, he knows that his opportunity has arrived. Forgetting his condition, he begins to stir in his position.

Paul speaks in a loud voice; it is a command. Now that the faith connection has been made, Paul is speaking directives, not requests. It seems as if Paul is speaking to the man's feet, but he is actually speaking to the man's faith. Sometimes you have to speak encouraging words to your own faith. The Apostle commands the man's faith to do what his legs and feet have never done [his feet could not go where his faith wouldn't take him]. It is faith that moves mountains, and "faith cometh by hearing, and hearing by the word of God." **[Romans 10:17]**

You may be going through the same thing. The years of lameness drained the man's' strength and dissolved his ability to see himself changed. His mind was darkened. He saw himself only as a lame man, but God saw him differently. When the power of God connects with the man's faith, *light* begins invading the dark places of his mind. God's Word brings light to the dark places in our understanding. The place within the man that has never lived, that had gone dark begins to experience light. He starts to see himself in a way that he has never before envisioned. We do not do anything that we do not first *visualize* in our minds. Visualization is so habitual and happens so quickly that we often do not notice it.

The place of visualization was dark in the lame man's mind. He saw others walking, and he thought about walking, but he could not "SEE" himself moving. Paul begins speaking to his faith, knowing that faith will bring light to his vision of himself and that he will begin to see himself walking. By watching others, he knows that there is something that God has equipped him to do that lies dormant (hidden, not active, dead) within him.

Paul's vision of the man's healing forces light into the lame man's vision of himself. Through the eyes of faith, the apostle sees him healed before he receives his healing. Paul probably smiled in anticipation because he saw him without his lameness, breaking through the barrier of his disability, receiving strength to be loosed from the place of his confinement.

Review and claim your scriptures every time doubt comes to your mind and speak faith declarations about you and your healing! Do the reverse of Mark 4:15 and steal the devils word immediately and replace it with the Word of God, your precious promises—2 Peter 1:1-4. Remember the devil is after your faith and he wants you to believe in his ability to defeat the Word of God in your life. Do not fall for that lie! The minute you begin to sense discouragement, catch yourself, recognize what's going on, and immediately speak out the truth of God's Word.

SPEAK:

> Discouragement you are a lie—because I am a child of God, He loves me; I am the object of His affection.
>
> The Bible says no weapon formed against me will prosper (Isaiah 54:17).
>
> My body is the temple of the Holy Spirit (1 Corinthians 6:19)
>
> Through Jesus I am an overcomer. Health and healing is in me now and is at work bringing forth the action of the Word of Life—the Word of God.
>
> I am free from degeneration; I am under the law of regeneration in Christ Jesus!" Amen.

Right now, **those who are reading this book, I speak to your faith, not your condition. Whatever you are facing cannot stand against faith in God. I declare strength to your faith and light to the dark places in your life experiences. By faith, God is creating light in the places that trial, testing, and disappointment have made dark.**

Again, I am not speaking to your dysfunction; I am speaking to your faith. God's rule is, *"According to your faith be it unto you."* [**Matthew 9:29**]. Not according to your condition. Amen? *"Have faith in God."*

[**Mark 11:22**] Whenever you respond by faith an entirely new realm of possibilities opens up to you. God wants to re-establish your potential while revealing His brand new possibilities for your life. Get this in your spirit, just because you've never done it before, does not mean you never will. Now is the time of your deliverance. Stand up!

Get back up in your faith and take hold of the blessings of the Word of God in an aggressive, proactive manner. You are more than a conqueror! You are a child of God! You are destined to win, and you were not created to lose. You are the recipient of His grace (all He is and all that He has). We've been made free from the curse of the law. We are a special people anointed by Him to rule and reign on this earth. God has big plans for you, so do not allow sickness or disease to put a stop to them. Take a firm hold on the blessings of the Lord today; take hold of your possessions in Jesus Christ.

Father God,

I speak your word into my circumstance(s) and I cling to your promises in Jesus' name.

Amen.

FROM THIS CHAPTER, I BELIEVE GOD'S PRESCRIPTION FOR ME IS:

_____

_____

_____

_____

_____

_____

_____

_____

_____

_____

_____

_____

CHAPTER 4

The Engrafted Word

Psalm 19:7 "The law of the Lord is perfect, converting the soul: the testimony of the Lord is sure, making wise the simple." God's Word is the perfect spiritual law! It is supernatural medicine. These are the Words the Spirit of the Lord revealed to me; **"You must speak God's Word to your individual circumstance or situation—someone else cannot do it for you."**

Let's look at James 1:21; *"Wherefore lay apart all filthiness and superfluity of naughtiness, and receive with meekness the engrafted word which is able to save your souls."*

When God's Word becomes *engrafted* {connected, stuck to} or *infused* into your spirit it has become a part of you. It cannot be separated from you. It is not only your thought and affirmation, it is you! It is The Word made flesh [John 1:14]. When this happens your flesh will reflect the life of the Word. When God's Word concerning healing takes root in your flesh, it becomes greater than any disease and healing is the result. The image that Word creates in you is already a reality in the spirit realm. When you speak God's Word from your heart, then faith gives substance to and activates the promises of God [Hebrews 11:1]. **Your faith frames your world daily!**

In Genesis Chapter 1 notice that every time God spoke; creation took place. Words are "carriers of faith"—**SEEDS!** The worlds were framed by the Word of God [Hebrews 11:3]. Without words, there wouldn't have been any creation. Your words create images and eventually you will live out the reality of that image. Every time you speak your faith, it creates a stronger image inside you.

A healing image is created by God's Word and your continual affirmation and agreement with it. Eventually that image will be perfected by the Word of God and you will begin to see yourself well. When the Word is engrafted into you, it infuses its life into you [John 6:63, Romans 8:11].

ENGRAFTED FAITH POSSESS REALITY

In Mark 5:25-28; the woman with the issue of blood said, *"If I may touch but his garments, I shall be whole."* She continued to speak until she saw herself well! Her "hope" was her goal, no matter how she felt. But she began filling hope with faith-filled words... *"I shall be restored to health."*

She was filling her hope with a faith image. She set her own point of contact to receive her healing. Her words penetrated her spirit and she began to SEE herself healed. Faith-filled words came from her mouth. Her degree of faith touched His clothing and thus made a demand on the covenant of God and the anointing that was upon Jesus. Her faith talking became the substance of her hope and her words became a living reality.

Faith gave substance to her hope and healing was manifested in her body. Remember, faith is the substance of things hoped for [Hebrews 11:1]. Hope lacks substance until filled with faith. Hope is only a goal-setter. Her hope was to be healed, but hope did not heal her, faith gave substance to her hope. Her faith gave substance to and brought about the manifestation of healing that was already hers because of the covenant. But **she had to call it!** Believing and calling for things that are not yet manifest. Giving voice to your faith in God's Word can also make you whole [Mark 5:34].

In Matthew 9:29 Jesus said; *"...according to your faith be it done unto you."* It is by "your faith" that brings about the manifestation. Command your faith to rise up!

God's Word is creative power. The worlds were framed by the Word of God. Confessing the Word of God can change your world. It takes discipline and commitment. Confess the Word audibly over your body. Psalm 107:19-20 tells us that we can always find supernatural hope from God's Word.

Speak blessings over your body, and speak in line with the Word of God regarding your situation—do not focus on and speak the problem— focus on and speak the answer. Your words are powerful—see Mark 11:23-24. We do not deny that sickness or disease is present, however we deny it the right to stay!

Example: "Sickness/disease, you have no right to stay in my body, 1 Peter 2:24 tells me that by the stripes laid upon Jesus, I was (past tense) healed. I agree with the Word and call my body healed in Jesus Name. I command you to go, you have no place here. Body, I call you blessed in Jesus Name. I call you strong, vibrant and healthy—permeated with and full of the life of God."

Father God,

I pray thy kingdom come thy will be done in my situation(s) as it is in heaven in Jesus' name.

Amen

FROM THIS CHAPTER, I BELIEVE GOD'S PRESCRIPTION FOR ME IS:

_____

_____

_____

_____

_____

_____

_____

_____

_____

_____

_____

_____

CHAPTER 5

Praying the Father's Will Into the Earth as it is in Heaven.

"*Thy kingdom come! Thy will be done in earth, as it is in heaven!*" [Matthew 6:10] Words act as containers, and contained within the words of this potent prophetic decree is the spiritual substance that shall bring it to pass in its' fullness!

So, what does THY KINGDOM COME mean? Obviously it speaks of HIS Kingdom, and the Kingdom is simply an extension of the identity of the King. The word translated as "kingdom" is basileia in Greek. Thayer's Greek Lexicon includes this definition: 1) *royal power, kingship, dominion, rule;* 1a) *not to be confused with an actual kingdom but rather the right or authority to rule over a kingdom.*

It is important to understand the latter part of that definition. Many in Christendom today are looking for a literal Kingdom, the New Jerusalem, to somehow fall from the sky. Perhaps we have seen a too many science fiction movies!

Genesis 1:26 says that God gave us the dominion over the earth to subdue [take control of] it [v.28]. The Kingdom of God is the power, the dominion, the right and authority to rule over a kingdom; even if that kingdom is sickness and disease. The Kingdom is IN the Holy Spirit, and the Holy Spirit is IN us! *"For the Kingdom of God is not meat and drink; but righteousness, and peace, and joy IN the Holy Ghost."* [Romans 14:17] *"Neither shall they say, Lo here! Or, lo there! For, behold, the Kingdom of God is WITHIN you."* [Luke 17:21]

So when we pray, "Thy kingdom come," we must not look for some abstract external event. We must understand the way the Kingdom has entrance into this natural earthly realm is THROUGH US!

"Thy will be done in earth, as it is in heaven." The word translated as **"WILL"** in this phrase is thelema in Greek. Its meanings include- *a determination, specifically purpose, decree; abstractly volition.* **Our Father already has a WILL, a purpose, a DECREE over everything!**

With an understanding of what His will is, we can move on in the verse; **"...be done in earth, as it is in heaven."** The word translated as "be done" is ginomai in Greek, its meaning includes- *to cause to be;* it is the "gen" in the English word generate, *to become or come into being, be brought (to pass), be fulfilled.* As we pray thy will be done, it is a creative declaration that reaches into the spiritual realm and serves as a catalyst for His will to be "gen"-erated, a spiritual genesis established in earth, thus causing it to be manifested in the natural realm. It is much more than just wishful thinking! It is a creative genesis!

Now we move on to a fascinating paradigm shift in our thinking; **"... in earth, as it is in heaven."** You would think that in translation where you have two different words in the same sentence you would translate them as different words. Here you have two uses of the English word **"in"** in the same sentence; however they are two different words in Greek. The word translated as "in" in the phrase **"in earth"** is epi in Greek. This is not the usual word for "in" that we find in Greek. The word translated as "in" in the phrase **"in heaven"** is en in Greek. The Greek word **epi** *is a primary preposition properly meaning SUPERIMPOSITION [place or lay one thing over another] of time, place, order, etc.]*

So when we decree over our body, Thy will be done IN earth, what we are really declaring is this- Thy will be gen-erated, creating a new genesis in this natural realm and SUPERIMPOSED upon the earth. When I look at it in this light it makes me think of **overshadowing.**

"While He yet spake, behold, a bright cloud overshadowed them: and behold a voice out of the cloud, which said, This is My beloved Son, in whom I am well pleased; hear ye Him.... And when they had lifted up their eyes, they saw NO MAN, save Jesus ONLY." [Matthew 17:5, 8]

The result of this overshadowing was this- they saw NO MAN, they saw Jesus ONLY! Father, our prayer is that we might see a complete OVERSHADOWING of heaven in earth that in ALL things Christ, and Christ alone would be seen!

The word translated as **"earth"** is ge (pronounced ghay) in Greek. It means soil; *by extension a region, or the solid part or the whole of the terrene globe (including the occupants in each application):—country, ground, land, world.* When I pray, "Thy will be done in earth, as it is in heaven.", I am decreeing that His will be superimposed upon the literal earth, that His Will be superimposed upon the natural realm! Yes, His Will is a spiritual thing but it must ultimately be manifested in this natural realm.

See, there's no sickness in heaven. When we pray for His will to be done in earth as it is in heaven -- **His Will must be superimposed upon the natural realm, in the SAME MANNER as His Will IS a FIXED POSITION in heaven.**

Father God,

Thank you that your word is like fire and it breaks every one of my problems into pieces, in Jesus' name.

Amen

FROM THIS CHAPTER, I BELIEVE GOD'S PRESCRIPTION FOR ME IS:

_____

_____

_____

_____

_____

_____

_____

_____

_____

_____

_____

_____

Robin McCray

CHAPTER 6

The Sledge Hammer - The Word of God

Jeremiah 23:29 says; *"Is not my word like a fire? Says the Lord, "And like a hammer that breaks every rock in pieces."*

For many months during my toughest hours and the pain increasing, the Spirit of the Lord revealed to me that *faith for healing is often times much like breaking concrete.* We are burdened down with the reality of the sickness or disease. The symptoms are very real and may have been well established, having been there for quite a while, and as we begin to stand on the Word of God, sometimes it can seem as if the problem is as hard as concrete, resisting our every swing of the sledgehammer of God's Word.

Learn to use the authority, which has been given to you by the Lord, to not only come against the sickness/disease, but to also run off any doubt and oppression that may be harassing you. Lay your hands on yourself and command the sickness to leave, command your body to line up with the Word of God. Tell doubt and unbelief and mental questioning to go in the Name of Jesus! Say, "I am a believer and not a doubter!!! I am a person of faith, I believe the Word." Luke 10:19, Isaiah 54:17, Mark 11:

Make praise and worship an everyday part of your life—rejoicing at the promises and for your life in Christ. He truly deserves our adoration, for He is our everything, and He has given us the victory! 1 Corinthians 15:57, 1 John 5:4. Praise and worship will help you to be victory minded. ***"The Lord is enthroned amongst the praises of His people"***—Psalm 22:3

Rejoice always, pray without ceasing, in everything give thanks for this is the will of God in Christ Jesus for you. 1 Thessalonians 5:16-18 NKJV

In the above verse, take note that it says "in" everything give thanks—it did not say "for" everything give thanks. In the midst of the trial, in the midst of the attack, when you feel as if the enemy is in your face with all of hell itself, right there, at that moment do not give in to the pressure of the devil, instead turn the tables on him and put the pressure back on the devil where it belongs and lift your hands to the Lord and begin to just love on God and praise and worship Him. (It'll just give the devil fits!)

Hebrews 13:15-16 tells us: *"Therefore by Him let us continually offer the sacrifice of praise to God, that is, the fruit of our lips, giving thanks to His name."* When is it a sacrifice to praise the Lord? When you do not feel like it—when the pressures on and heat is turned up real high!

So sing to Him, praise Him, love on Him for your salvation and for the Holy Spirit He has sent to live within you, who is your comforter and your teacher, the one who is right there with you now. Praise Him for the precious promises in His Word that He has given to you that will never fail. Praise Him for the ongoing refining work that He is constantly bringing about within you. Praise Him because He is the author and the finisher of your faith. Praise Him—you are The King's Kid, you are an heir of God and a joint heir with Jesus Christ. Praise Him because He has risen you up and seated you with Jesus in the Heavenly realms. Praise Him now that He has made you More Than a Conqueror in Christ Jesus. Praise Him, for His banner over us is love and love never fails.

We can grow tired, discouraged and even be tempted to give up. What you may not realize is, just like the concrete, though you may not see any changes, *it is beginning to crystallize and lose structural integrity from within;* therefore getting ready to shatter. Every stroke of the hammer [the Word of God] brings it closer to the point where it will eventually crumble. We need to come to the place of understanding that the Word of God is all powerful. You cannot separate the Word of God from the God of the Word. They are one in the same. John 1:14 says *"...and the word became flesh and dwelt among us."*

The Word of God is a fire that purges and melts away all impurities, just as fire purifies precious metal, leaving only that which is treasured. It is also a *hammer* that is able to crush even the most resistant stubborn circumstances, even those that seem so hard that they could never be removed. The Word of God is what it is—the very Word of God! The question is not in the ability of the Word, it is in our perception of it. Persistence breaks down resistance!

Take a break if you are tired and worn out in the illness. What I encourage you to do is take a praise and worship break instead of a pity party. A praise party will refresh you with His power and might. Once you have been renewed take hold of the sledgehammer—God's healing Word—with renewed vigor and strength, and command the problem to leave in Jesus' Name. Get your healing scriptures and stare the problem square in the face and tell it what the Word says concerning your victory. Make it personal, put your name in those scriptures, knowing He did it all just for you, and would have done it just the same way if you were the only one who would have benefitted from His going to the Cross.

Praise Him—He is your healer, your sanctifier, your peace, your provider, your Shepherd. Read through Psalm 23 and 91 and get happy at what your God has promised and is going to do for you. Allow the joy of the Lord to well up on the inside of you, because after all, the Joy of the Lord IS your strength!! !

As you do this, you will sense the very atmosphere around you begin to change. Why? Because you have made a choice to put the focus of your attention on to the Lord instead of rehearsing your problem over and over in your mind; fueled by the enemy and his despair. You have made a decision to exalt the Lord and His ways through praise, by faith, no matter what you see and feel. Make praise a part of your daily life and you will never be the same—*ever!!!*

Dear God,

Thank you Lord that I am no longer under the curse but I have been delivered and set free because of the blood, in Jesus' name!

Amen

FROM THIS CHAPTER, I BELIEVE GOD'S PRESCRIPTION FOR ME IS:

_____

_____

_____

_____

_____

_____

_____

_____

_____

_____

_____

_____

CHAPTER 7

Free from the Curse

In the Book of John, (chapter nine) is an interesting lesson regarding healing and the blessings that are offered to us through Jesus Christ as Lord. This story is of a blind man that Jesus and His disciples were passing. Upon noticing him, the disciples questioned Jesus as to why this man was blind. *"Master, who sinned, this man or his parents that he was born blind?" Jesus replied, "Neither this man nor his parents sinned but the works of God should be revealed in him."*

Jesus explained that the sickness was not due to a specific sin of the man or his parents, but is a result of the effect of the curse that is in the world. The entrance of sin; from the original fall of man in the Garden of Eden, [Genesis 3: 1 – 19] led to sickness, disease, affliction and death. Jesus was saying that because of that fallen condition, the power of God is present and available to the man and as far as God is concerned, Jesus stated in a rather matter-of-fact manner, *"It should be revealed in him!"* **"Revealed"** in the Greek means: to be manifested, displayed and illustrated.

Jesus then spat on the ground and made a new set of eyes from the clay and saliva—Jesus was disgusted with sin and the curse that had alienated mankind from true fellowship with God and had caused so much suffering in the world.

God is love, absolute love—the highest and purest form of love that could ever exist. One of the attributes of love—it cannot keep from giving out its goodness. It is always reaching out. Jesus spat on the ground with intensity and disgust, with the clear knowing of His purpose that He came into the world to free mankind from the bonds of sin [John 3:8]. Jesus was saying: *"Curse you have no hold over me, for I am Love, Light and Life and I have come to expel the works of darkness."* He took the clay made from the earth [Genesis 3:17] symbolizing the curse, anointed or placed it on the blind man's eyes and said to him; "Go wash in the Pool of Siloam."

We are anointed to be free and to live in liberty, free from the curse and its effects, for this is the gift of God, eternal and abundant life [John 10:10]. The power and life of God is about to be made manifest in the earth. *Siloam* is translated as "Sent" and is symbolic of *the Messiah the Sent and Anointed One* that was to come. It was a prophetic act, sending Him to that pool, foreshadowing that all of mankind will have the right to the freedom and cleansing that comes through Him.

In Luke 4:18-19; *"...he has sent me to heal..."* "Sent" is the root word Apostello in Greek which means *to be set apart for a mission or purpose, to be sent, to be appointed for something,* confirming the fact that Jesus is the true Apostle and Sent One, our Messiah. The goal of His purpose: *to set at liberty those who are oppressed,* "to set" (same word) is used to describe Jesus' purpose.

What Isaiah [Isaiah 61:1-3] was prophesying and Jesus was proclaiming, is through Jesus, the Messiah, the Sent One, through His redemptive work, we who are recipients of His grace, have been set apart, and are appointed for liberty and freedom from oppression (that includes sickness and disease). **Liberty** means *deliverance, a freeing from anything that had or has a hold on us.*

It is pure *justification because of the blood that was made for an atonement of our sins that put us in position of His righteousness.* In this state of righteousness, no sickness, disease or sin-caused malady [disease or ailment] in any area of the body, soul or spirit has any right to stay in us! We are anointed and appointed, apostles, set apart in His righteousness. Not just to experience it for ourselves, but given a mandate to take it to the world itself, testifying of His great grace and love for mankind. That's our mission, that's our purpose—to spread the Good News of a loving, compassionate God. Luke 4:19 says; *"...to proclaim the acceptable year of the Lord."*

The barrier that sin caused broke our right to fellowship with the Lord and has been removed. We now have the right to come boldly to the Throne of Grace, to obtain mercy and find grace to help in a time of need [Hebrews 4:16].

Take a bold new stand today with your faith, Jesus is your Jubilee. He has paid the price for your freedom and set you apart, anointed you and appointed you to receive all that He is and all that He has for you to live in daily. He is your refreshing. He is your life, and He is your abundance of grace, life, mercy and love. It is your birthright as a Believer; makeup your mind and set your will that you will not be denied. Allow this great truth to go deep and build your faith, rise up in a new attitude of hope and take hold of what Jesus did for you. Jubilee is a done deal—it is already bought and paid for and has your name stamped on it.

Understand this—**it is biblically illegal for the enemy to bind you any longer.** Know this: the enemy can only have or possess the ground that you allow him to have. This is why it is so important for you to know the truth, to know the Word—which is the documentation of your covenant rights. So rise up and take your stand and take back what rightfully belongs to you. The bonds have been broken, the Gospel trumpet of Jubilee has sounded, and it is time for you to stand up and take hold of your rightful possession in Him—you are anointed and appointed, you are an apostle to victory. Amen!!!!

Father God,

I AGREE WITH YOUR heal-ing, delivering and liberating WORD CONCERNING MY SITUATION! I await its mani-festation, in Jesus name!

Amen

FROM THIS CHAPTER, I BELIEVE GOD'S PRESCRIPTION FOR ME IS:

_____

_____

_____

_____

_____

_____

_____

_____

_____

_____

_____

_____

CHAPTER 8

Agree with God

If ye abide in me, and my words abide in you, ye shall ask what ye will, and it shall be done unto you. [JOHN 15: 7]

The Bible is God's Word to us. It is the operator's manual, given to mortal men by an eternal God. God and His Word are alive and inseparable. His Word does not change, nor can it fail, nor will it return unto Him without accomplishing what it was sent to do [Isaiah 55:11].

When you confess what God's Word says about you, you are *agreeing* that what He has said concerning you is true. There is infinite power in that agreement. Decree that you have what God says you have. Proclaim that you are who God says you are. God said He would hasten after His Word to perform it, to bring it to pass in your life. When you speak the Word, angels hearken to that command [Psalm 103:20], and all of heaven will back you up. You have a written guarantee...His Word.

SAY THIS: GOD, I BELIEVE WHAT YOU SAID IN THE WORD. I KNOW THAT YOUR WORD IS LIFE AND TRUTH. I WILL COMMAND ALL THAT YOU HAVE SPOKEN BY THE POWER OF YOUR SPIRIT. AMEN.

RETURNING GOD'S WORD TO HIM

God declares that His Word will not return to Him void [Isaiah 55:11]. We are to return His Word by *giving voice to it,* and He will create the fruit if our lips [Isaiah 57:19]. Confessing God's Word is a way you can fellowship with the Lord and increase your faith at the same time. Do not let it become a hit and miss proposition. Make it a practice to take God's medicine on a regular basis, just as you would any other medicine. Then it will bring life to you and health to your flesh [Proverbs 4:20-22].

The key: **calling things that are not as though they were.** In Romans 4:17-22; Abraham became fully persuaded that God would do what He had promised. The way he became fully persuaded was by calling those things which were not manifested as though they were. God uses spiritual forces which are not seen to nullify natural things that are seen. When it comes to divine healing this is a vital principal. We should declare to ourselves what God's Word reveals about us, regardless of the circumstances or how we feel about it.

In Romans 10:6-8; notice the Word is first in your mouth and (then) in your heart. God's Word becomes engrafted into your heart as you speak it. There is nothing more important to your faith than declaring what God has said about you with your own voice. Giving voice to God's Word is a method of calling for things that God has given by promise and is not yet manifested.

You are *establishing [setting up, initiating or bring about]* what God had said to be true concerning healing even though it is not yet a reality in your body. *God has also given us all things that pertain to life and godliness* [2 Peter 1:3]. By mixing faith with God's Word, you are calling for the promise of God to be manifested in your body. This will cause you to be fully persuaded, and healing is the result. You are simply *proclaiming* what God has said in His Word to be a fact, regardless of your present condition.

You are calling your body well according to Luke 17:5-6 and Mark 11:23. **Your body is listening to you and it will obey you if you believe and not doubt in your heart.** Your words have more effect on your body than anyone else's words. Your body was created with the ability to heal itself, and if every part functions properly, it will. See, some sickness is caused by a chemical imbalance in the body, and the part of the brain that controls the speech also controls the secretion of chemicals to the body. I beseech you to "agree" with the what the Word of God says concerning your healing. Don't agree with what you' re feeling in your body. Don't be moved by what you're feeling; be moved by what the Word says; "By whose stripes you were healed." I Peter 2:24b.

Father,

I call forth healing into my body and circumstance(s) in Jesus' name!

Amen

FROM THIS CHAPTER, I BELIEVE GOD'S PRESCRIPTION FOR ME IS:

_____

_____

_____

_____

_____

_____

_____

_____

_____

_____

_____

_____

CHAPTER 9

Call What You Want

Call for "positive" things, even though they are not yet a reality in your body. Call them until they are manifested. You have a God-given right to exercise authority over your body. Paul tells us in Romans 8:13... *"if you live after the flesh you shall die; but if you through the Spirit do mortify the deeds of the body, you shall live."* Your spirit, if trained properly, wants to say it the way God said it in His Word. Your body will respond to the demands of the human spirit. **If you feed the spirit man God's Word, it will make demands on the flesh to line up with the Word of God.** You must make a demand on it before it will respond. The truth is, your body always responds to your words in some manner, either for better or worse. So choose your words carefully.

In Mark 11:13-24; Jesus spoke to a fig tree having no leaves and cursed it. Peter and the other disciples passed by later seeing the fig tree that Jesus cursed earlier withered away. Jesus told them *"...you can have what you say in faith..."* God created man's body to live forever, but sin brought the curse of sickness and death. The human body has an inherent ability to heal itself. God's Word is the original and most powerful medicine available yesterday, today and forever. Certain medicines and chemicals will only "aid" the body in the healing process.

God's Word is the *original* and most powerful medicine available today. It is the **original medicine** sent for the specific purpose of healing. **It was His "Word" that created the human body.** In Genesis 1:26 says; *"And God said, Let us make man in our image, after our likeness..."* and in Genesis 1:27 *"And God created man in his own image..."*

Psalm 107:20 says; *"He sent His word and healed them, and delivered them from their destruction."* Luke 17:6 says *"...it would obey you."* Always remember this; when you are sick, call yourself well, for you are calling for what you do not have. Put this into practice and make it a way of life, then your body will respond to your faith demands that are based on the authority of God's Holy Word. It will not happen just because you say it, but saying it is involved in causing it to happen. Saying it is the way you plant the "seeds" for what your "need." The spoken Word of God imparts spirit life into your physical body [John 6:63], for His Word is the *incorruptible* seed and it produces after its kind.

MIRACLE IN YOUR MOUTH

Effective faith must be active and *functioning* with two separate areas of our being, and it is more than believing only in our heart. Faith is a true *action* word [James 2:26]. Faith requires action. I am not talking about a "works trip." We must realize that real faith, the kind that brings results is *proactive* and *assertive.* Faith comes when you are exposed to truth.

Romans 10:6-11 makes it very clear to see that when appropriating faith, we need to have it *functioning* and *working together harmoniously* in both places, in our mouth and in our heart. The word "salvation" you will find that this word speaks just as strongly of healing, in the present as it does of eternal life. *"For with the heart one believes unto righteousness (being right or whole), and with the mouth confession is made unto salvation/healing."* We need the heart (believing, being convinced with a knowing faith) and the mouth (speaking out, declaring what the Word says) work-ing together. Generally, either one used alone will not bring about the desired results.

Our words play an important role in our lives and all the more when we are speaking the Word of God over our situation. No, it is not mind over matter—it is the Word over the matter. Learn not to focus on the problem but instead focus on the answer.

Continually speaking out how bad things are will not bring about relief, it is only a declaration of what is. But *speaking* and *laying claim* to the Word of God will bring about the desired change. It is an exchange of the natural for the supernatural. We are extension of God in situations. Speak it!

In Ephesians 6:17; *"...and the sword of the Spirit, which is the word of God."* Note the Greek word for "word" here is Rhema which means the spoken word. The Word of God is a sword when it comes out of your mouth.

In Revelation 19:15; see the sword coming out of the mouth of Je-sus—the SPOKEN WORD. Speak the Word over your situation until you have what the Word says and it will activate the "angels" on your behalf [Psalm 103:20-21].

In Mark 11:23; *"...whosoever shall say unto this mountain, Be thou re-moved and be thou cast into the sea..."* NOTE: Words are a vehicle of releasing our faith. Speak to your "mountain" or "obstacle" and command it to be removed.

In Job 22:28; *"Thou shalt also decree a thing, and it shall be established unto thee: and the light shall shine upon you."* NOTE: Dare to take God at His Word and lay claim to the covenant promises and boldly declare to the devil and hell that you will not be held down by your present situation, but you will instead have the reality of the blessing established within you! Say it out loud! One of the most powerful things you can do is set your will in line with the Word of God.

Isaiah 57:19; *"I create the fruit of the lips; Peace, peace to him that is far off, and to him that is near, saith the LORD, and I will heal him."* NOTE: He is saying: "I create the 'fruit' of the lips. What kind of fruit is proceeding from your mouth? Are you giving the Lord words (substance) that He can work with, which is His Word? See Isaiah 55:11…He said, His Word would not return to Him void. How does it return? When we speak it (give voice).

Psalm 91:1-2 says *"He that dwelleth in the secret place of the most High shall abide under the shadow of the Almighty: I will say of the LORD, He is my refuge and my fortress: my God: in him will I trust."* Notice the principle and the important role words play in taking hold of the promises, security and deliverance of God. In the beginning of this Psalm, the Psalmist speaks out making bold (confidence) faith declarations, laying claim to his covenant with God, through his words.

Immediately, in the beginning of your circumstances or trials, get your faith into motion by declaring who God is to you and what He has promised to do for you. Make the Word your beginning in every area in life [John 1:1].

It is so important to lay claim to the Scriptures *personally*, declaring them in the first tense, inserting your name in them where it is applicable and boldly declaring that the promises already belongs to you and you have it now!

FATHER GOD,

Thank you that your word is life to every dead situation in my life in Jesus' name!

Amen

FROM THIS CHAPTER, I BELIEVE GOD'S PRESCRIPTION FOR ME IS:

_____

_____

_____

_____

_____

_____

_____

_____

_____

_____

_____

_____

_____

CHAPTER 10

There was a Noise

In the book of Ezekiel, Chapter 7 we find the story of the *valley of dry bones*. In verses 1 through 2; we must take notice of the condition of the bones; they were "very" dry. They had been there for quite some time, baked by the scorching sun day in and day out. They were brittle, parched and cracked, any and all life had long since passed away. They were situated in the "valley", which represents a low place of existence. You may be feeling as if you are stuck in the middle of the valley of despair. Life faded away and your present condition may seem to be so dry and lifeless.

Notice in verse 3. Remember who is asking the question, the Giver of all life, the Creator of heaven and earth, the One who is all wise. Ezekiel responds, "You know Lord, and I am open and waiting for your instruction." With that answer and the Spirit of Faith, the door is now opened wide for a miracle to take place. In verses 4 through 6, the Lord gives Ezekiel the plan of attack. The Lord told Ezekiel to do something that did not make sense to his mind, to speak, not only that, but he was told to speak the Word of the Lord to them!

In Ezekiel 37:7-8; Ezekiel went beyond his natural reasoning, did as he was commanded (he obeyed), and there was a noise. The bones assembled themselves together and formed men—flesh and all! God said to do it, Ezekiel did and an unusual miracle took place! Maybe the Lord is telling you to do something strange and it does not make sense in the natural. Will you obey? The Lord told Ezekiel to "prophesy" to the bones.

In Revelation 19:10; an angel is giving instructions to John: *"The testimony of Jesus is the spirit of prophecy."* The Bible reveals to us that Jesus is the Living Word of God [John 1:1, 14]. Jesus and the Word of God are One. So when the Scriptures says, "the testimony of Jesus is the spirit of prophecy," we could also understand this to read that "the testimony of the Word is the spirit of prophecy" as well.

This action always begins in the "spirit" and if we will refuse to give up or change our belief and confession, our miracle of life will eventually begin to materialize within our natural situation. Once you understand this, then you'll know it is just a matter of time. John 6:63 tells us that *"It is the Spirit who gives life, the flesh profits nothing. The words that I speak to you are "Spirit" and they are Life."*

The problem—We do not usually "hear" the noise or realize the action or beginning results when we speak or prophesy or reveal the Word of God, the testimony of Jesus to our situation, our mountains, or our obstacle.

Daniel 10:12-13, 19 *"...Since the 1st day that you set your mind to gain understanding and to humble yourself before your God, your words were heard, and I have come in response to them. But the (evil/demonic) prince of the Persian kingdom resisted me 21 days. Then Michael, one of the chief (angelic) princes, came to help me, because I was detained there with the king of Persia..."Do not be afraid, O man highly esteemed," he said. "Peace. Be strong now; be strong."*

Remember, it takes 9 months to grow a baby after conception, so does it often take time for your answer or healing to manifest itself. Believe that God is working on your behalf as He and His staff battle out in the unseen realm on your behalf.

Remember, Christ did not rescue Himself. He allowed God to rescue Him at the right time. "Take **God** at His word. Accept **your healing** as already) accomplished. So **wait** on the Lord; never consider it a waste of time.

Remember what Jesus said in Mark 11:23. Do not try to figure it out, just simply "obey" what Jesus said and act upon it. Stand firm in your confession and belief of the Word of God, and watch God move on your behalf.

Galatians 6:9 says; *"And let us not be weary in well doing: for in due season we shall reap, if we faint not."* Do not settle for just a partial miracle! Get the whole thing, stay with it and continue to speak the Word over it until your situation becomes exactly how the Word says it should be.

Use your God–given authority in Christ Jesus and command life, speak life; reveal life—which is the truth, to your situation. Begin to lay claim to them (promises) with new life and a fresh assurance. Know that what God has promised in His Word for you is also His will for you. Begin to command the troubled area to line up with the Word and prophesy (reveal) what God has said in His Word regarding your situation. Amen!

Cast off discouragement! Stay with it and continue to SPEAK THE WORD and remember to praise Him for it as well. And as you do, have a heart of knowing that: there is always a noise of action in response to the proclaiming of God's Word, ALWAYS! Whether you hear it or not, God is working in response to His Word, He said so! Jeremiah 1:12 *"Then said the Lord to me, you have seen well, for I am alert and active, watching over My Word to perform it."* (Amplified)

Father God,

Your word brings life to every area of my life! I welcome your life in mine, in Jesus name.

Amen

FROM THIS CHAPTER, I BELIEVE GOD'S PRESCRIPTION FOR ME IS:

_____

_____

_____

_____

_____

_____

_____

_____

_____

_____

_____

_____

CHAPTER 11

Let the Word of God Become Life

Some Christians may say "I just cannot seem to memorize the Scriptures in the Word of God. I've tried but I just cannot seem to get any of them to stick with me." The problem is very common to many Christians; the Word has not yet become life to them.

The Word of God tells us in Proverbs 4:20-22; *"My son, give attention to my words; incline your ear to my sayings. Do not let them depart from your eyes; For they are "life" to those who find them, and health to all their flesh."*

Verse 22 says the "word is life" to those that find it. It does not say that the Word is life to all, to those with a casual gaze; instead it becomes life to those with a serious intent, who will act upon it. It becomes life to those who take the time to dig in and locate them, cherish them and take them to heart for the precious promises of God that they truly are.

The Word of God is Life. That's what it is. The blessing is there just waiting for someone to come along and take hold of if, to internalize it and grab on to it with the arms of faith and not let go!

The first part of the block of Scripture [Proverbs 4:20], it describes a person who is "proactive" and "purposeful" with the Word. It reveals a person who recognizes the worth and riches contained within the Word, a person who has internalized the Word and has allowed it to sink down deep into their heart. This is a person, who has set aside time every day to read, research, ponder and meditate (chewed) on the Word of God. And the result is that the Word became life to them and it even affected their physical body becoming health (medicine to all of their flesh). Total Wholeness!

Jesus said in John 14:6; *"I am the way, the truth and the life."* The word "life"—"Zoe" means: Life that is the highest and best of which Christ is. Jesus does not have any sickness or disease, any poverty, fear or depression. Those things cannot stand in His presence. He is the purest form of all that is good. The purest of the pure, the best of the best!

In John 10:10b; *"I am come that they might have life, and that they might have it more abundantly. "* Jesus is saying, "I have come that you would share in and partake of My life, which is the highest and best of all that I have to offer, and that you would experience it to the fullest sense which is the will of God for you. It is His will that you experience it in the here and now! He is waiting for someone to believe it, receive it and act upon it so He can bring it to pass in their life.

Hebrews 4:12 tells us... *"The word of God is "living" and "powerful" and "sharper" than a two edged sword."* There is nothing that the life of the Word cannot deal with. It will perform spiritual surgery.

It will cut out sickness and disease and give you health. It will cut out poverty and bring you into abundance. It will cut out depression, anger and strife and bring you peace, life and joy. It will cut out hopelessness and give you purpose and expectancy once again. It will cut out failure and give you success. It will cut out the old ways of your life and give you newness of life—life to the fullest, overflowing.

In Matthew 4:4; Jesus said, *"Man shall not live by bread alone, but by every word that proceeds from the mouth of God."* The word "proceeds" is present tense and is saying, "that which is currently proceeding." God is speaking today and you will begin to hear His voice by continually being in the Word. Our survival depends upon it! It (the Word of God) is the prescribed way, designated by the Lord Himself, for the born-again Believer to thrive upon the earth. It needs to be taken in "daily", just as natural food. The Word of God is not just a "religious" book, it is "life", and it is not to be underestimated or neglected, it is to be highly treasured and esteemed for the precious life of which it is. It is "living" and when it is internalized, it germinates within your spirit and brings forth a harvest of blessing. It will heal your past, cause you to flourish in your moment, and provide for your future. The Word of God is Life—There's no other way!

Meditate on the Word of God over and over until it starts speaking back. By doing this you will never lose vision, in fact your vision will be enhanced and will grow and come into spiritually maturity [See Hebrews 12:1-3]. God's best waits just up ahead. It is there for those who will endure through the barren wilderness, enter in and take possession of it through faith and patience.

We are one with Christ. Sickness has no right in Him, so it has no legal right to us. It is illegal, off limits; it has no right to stay. Take a firm stand and run off the attack and lie of the enemy. You belong to Him; you are washed in His precious Blood, the covenant Blood. Command it to leave and insist on your rights now, and do not quit until it changes and becomes just as the Word says it should be. Keep going, do not stop! Look! You are coming to the top of another hill, could this be it? Do not get discouraged, your blessing could be just on the other side of the next hill. Build up your strength with the bread of the Word of God, and enjoy another refreshing drink from basking in His presence.

Set aside a time by yourself, daily, to fellowship with God. Make it a practice to meditate on His Word by speaking it to your body. Declare these Holy Scriptures to be true until you are fully persuaded. Remember, your body will respond to your voice; how much more will it respond to God's Word spoken in faith. Now take His prescription (His prescribed Word) on a daily basis as many times a day as you feel is necessary...go ahead you will not overdose and there are no side effects. Praise God!!!!!!

FROM THIS CHAPTER, I BELIEVE GOD'S PRESCRIPTION FOR ME IS:

_____

_____

_____

_____

_____

_____

_____

_____

_____

_____

_____

CHAPTER 12

Use your God-Given Authority and Resist Fear!

Healing is a blessing that the enemy does not want you to have. With this knowledge in hand, you must build your arsenal with weaponry that will allow you to march forward in your God-given authority while defeating the enemy and every strategy and tactic he may employ.

Here are some weapons to pull from your arsenal.

Matthew 18:18 *"Verily I say unto you, whatsoever ye shall bind on earth shall be bound in heaven: and whatsoever ye shall loose on earth, shall be loosed in heaven."* NOTE: The word "bind" means to forbid and "loose" means to let go or to allow to go free. Do not allow sickness, pain or disease run free in your body, bind it or forbid it to stay there any longer because of your rights as a Believer.

John 10:10b *"I am come that they might have life and that they might have it more abundantly."* NOTE: The desired will of the LORD for every Believer, that we experience abundant life "Zoë"- being the highest and best of which Christ is.

Luke 10:19 *"Behold, I give unto you power to tread on serpents and scorpions, and over all the power of the enemy: and nothing shall by any means hurt you."* NOTE: The word "power" meaning *authority*. Jesus said; He has given us authoritative power over all. Command sickness and disease to leave you NOW in the Name of Jesus.

Isaiah 54:17 *"No weapon that is formed against thee shall prosper; and every tongue that shall rise against thee in judgment thou shalt condemn. This is the heritage of the servants of the LORD, and their righteousness is of me, saith the LORD."* NOTE: Sickness is judging you falsely, it is your birthright to live in health, and you condemn it with the Word of God, and command it to leave your body in Jesus' Name.

1 John 4:4 *"Ye are of God, little children, and have overcome them: because greater is he that is in you, than he that is in the world."*

1 John 5:4 *"For whosoever is born of God overcometh the world: and this is the victory that overcometh the world, even our faith."* NOTE: Faith in God is victory all time.

John 17:14 *"I have given them thy word; and the world hath hated them, because they are not of the world, even as I am not of the world."* NOTE: We are not of this world. Sickness and disease and failure belong to this world. As a Believer, we are given the right to overcome that which comes against us by holding fast to the Word of God.

Romans 8:31 *"What shall we then say to these things? If God be for us, who can be against us?"* Say out loud: I am a winner; I am victorious through the Lord Jesus Christ. Begin to see yourself the way God sees you.

1 John 4:17 *"Herein in our love made perfect, that we may have boldness in the Day of Judgment: because as he is, so are we in this world."* NOTE: "That we may have 'boldness' now in this life in the face of adversity, knowing who we are in Christ, knowing what belongs to us in Him and tenaciously holding onto it. As He is, so are we in this world. How is He NOW? He is not sick, He is not diseased—it cannot touch Him, and we are His Body—the Body of Christ. Insist on having the blessing of the Lord manifested in you. Praise Him for it NOW and worship Him for His holiness.

2 Peter 1:3-4 *"According as his divine power hath given unto us all things that pertain unto life and godliness, through the knowledge of him that hath called us to glory and virtue."* NOTE: The word "has" given us all things that pertain to life. The blessing of health was purchased for is at the Cross, it belongs to you now. The importance of the Word of God, your healing must be rooted steadfastly on the Word, not on what you see or how you feel. His nature is total health and well being, EXPECT IT.

1Corinthians 1:9 *"God is faithful, by whom ye were called unto the fellowship of his Son Jesus Christ our Lord."* NOTE: God is faithful to His covenant Word. "Fellowship" is a strong covenant word. In Greek it means: intimacy, partnership and participator and also communion. We have been given the right to share intimately, in partnership and participation in His life. He is life, the purest form of life and He is called us to share intimately in it with Him. It is a place where sickness and disease have no right.

Romans 5:17 *"For by on man's (Adam) offence death reigned by one; much more they which receive abundance of grace and of the gift of righteousness shall reign in life by one, Jesus Christ."* NOTE: "Will reign in life"—this life in the here and now. Take hold of the victory that is yours through the Word.

Genesis 1:28 *"And God blessed them and God said unto them, be fruitful, and multiply, and replenish the earth, and subdue it: and have dominion over* *the fish of the sea, and over the fowl of the air, and over every living thing that moveth on the earth."* NOTE: Subdue [overcome, control, take charge] and have dominion over every living thing. God gave the blessing, He gave the command, He gave you the right—now do it! Put your foot down on sickness and disease and command it to go—it has no right to stay, you are a blood bough child of God.

Colossians 1:13 *"Who hath delivered us from the power of darkness, and hath translated us into the kingdom of his dear Son."* NOTE: The word "translated" or "conveyed" is to be transferred, removed out of one and place into another. The power of darkness [curse], no longer has a hold on you.

Proverbs 3:7-8 *"Be not wise in thine own eyes: fear the LORD, and depart from evil. It shall be health to thy navel, and marrow to thy bones."* NOTE: The word "fear the Lord" means to reverence and worship the Lord in all things.

Exodus 15:26 *"...If thou wilt diligently hearken to the voice of the LORD thy God, and wilt do that which is right in his sight, and wilt give ear to his commandments, and keep all his statues, I will put none of these diseases upon thee, which I have brought upon the Egyptians: for I am the LORD that healeth thee."* NOTE: "I am the Lord that healeth thee"—He is Jehovah Ropha!

Malachi 4:2-3 *"But unto you that fear my name shall the Sun of righteousness arise with healing in his wings; and ye shall go forth, and grow up as calves of the stall. And ye shall tread down the wicked; for they shall be ashes under the soles of your feet in the day that I shall do this, saith the LORD of hosts."* NOTE: Let this be a reality—"On the day that I do this" was at Calvary. Now the enemy is "ashes" under our feet and healing and protection belongs to us.

Psalm 30:2 *"O LORD my God, I cried unto thee, and thou hast healed me."*

Psalm 107:19-20 *"Then they cry unto the LORD in their trouble, and he saveth them out of their distresses. He sent His word, and healed them, and delivered them from their destructions."*

Matthew 7:7-8 *"Ask, and it shall be given to you; seek, and ye shall find, knock, and it shall be opened unto you: For every one that asketh receiveth;*

and he that seeketh findeth; and unto him that knocketh it shall be opened." NOTE: The word "ask" meaning of insistent asking with a knowing of what belongs to the one making the request. Present a solid requisition to God, knowing He longs to distribute what He has to the one in need. [Read James 1:5-8—we must ask in faith and faith always knows, it never wishes!]

Ezekiel 16:16 *"And when I passed by thee, and saw thee polluted [covered with] in thine own blood, I said unto thee when thou wast in thy blood, Live; yea, I said unto thee, when thou wast in thy blood, Live."*

2 Corinthians 1:20 *"For all the promises of God in him are yea, and in him Amen, unto the glory of God by us."*

Psalm 35:27 *"Let them shout for joy, and be glad, that favour my righteous cause: yea, let them say continually, Let the Lord be magnified, which hath pleasure in the prosperity of his servant."* NOTE: The word "prosperity" here is shalom [peace], which means health, prosperity and peace wholeness, welfare. God takes pleasure in the health of His children. Grab a hold of this!

How are your strength and your faith doing now? What wonderful medicine you have taken thus far! You can walk in complete wholeness because of the blood of Jesus knowing that your prescription is the Will of God and His blessing of goodness and health now!

Jeremiah 29:11 *"For I know the thoughts that I think toward you, saith the LORD, thoughts of peace, and not of evil, to give you an expected end."* NOTE: The word 'peace" is Shalom—the meaning of health and prosperity, which is His will. Begin to expect it!

Luke 12:32 *"Fear not, little flock, for it is you Father's good pleasure to give you the kingdom."* NOTE: Realize it gives God pleasure to give to you, He is a giver—so cast off fear—you are rich in Him. Receive it.

Psalm 121:7-8 *"The LORD shall preserve thee from all evil: he shall preserve thy soul. The LORD shall preserve thy going out and thy coming in from this time forth, and even for evermore."* NOTE: Notice He said He would keep or preserve us from all evil. Preserve means to guard, to keep, to hedge about, to protect, and to attend to. He promises to do this now and forevermore.

Hebrew 13:20-21 *"Now the God of peace that brought again from the dead our Lord Jesus, that great shepherd of the sheep, through the blood of the everlasting covenant. Make you perfect in every good work to do his will, working in you that which is well-pleasing in his sight, through Jesus Christ; to whom be glory forever and ever. Amen."* NOTE: Completeness and wholeness which is intended through the Blood Covenant. That you be strengthen, be made complete and be perfected, be made what you ought to be [because of the shed blood] and equipped with everything good so you can accomplish His will. Our God has a purpose and a plan for you and He wants you to accomplish it now in Jesus Name. This is His will.

Have you grasped hold of the fact that you can absolutely be healed in Jesus name? Have you embraced the fact that by His stripes you are healed? The Word of God brings healing. The Word of God is the same yesterday, today and forever. The Word of God is truth! Ingest his truth for your healing.

Psalm 119:50 *"This is my comfort in my affliction: for thy word hath quickened me."*

Romans 10:17 *"So then faith cometh by hearing, and hearing by the word of God."* NOTE: Faith for healing comes by hearing the Word of God. Allow your faith to be built up! [DAILY]

Proverbs 4:20-22 *"My son, attend to my words; incline thine ear to my sayings. Let them not depart from thine eyes; keep them in the midst of thine heart. For they are life unto those that find them, and health to all their flesh."* NOTE: The taken of God's Word is life and medicine to your flesh.

John 8:32 *"And you shall know the truth [God's Word], and the truth shall make you free."* NOTE: The Word of God is truth. Once you know the truth, then you can begin to exercise faith and expect the promises of God to manifest in you—and they will.

John 15:7 *"If you abide in me, and my words abide in you, ye shall ask what ye will, and it shall be done unto you."*

Jeremiah 23:29 *"Is not my word like as fire? saith the LORD; and like a hammer that breaketh every rock in pieces?"* NOTE: The Word of God is an all-consuming fire that will melt away and burn off that which is not of God and a powerful crushing force to break a part even the toughest and most stubborn circumstances. Continue taking the hammer of God's Word and continue to hit the situations in your life that are not of God, until they give way and become what the Word says they should be. Amen.

2 Timothy 3:16-17 *"All scripture is given by inspiration of God, and is profitable for doctrine, for reproof, for correction, for instruction in righteousness. That the man of God may be perfect, thoroughly furnished unto all good works."* NOTE: It is God's will that you be complete and thoroughly equipped for every good work. Know that God wants you to be able bodied.

Isaiah 55:11 *"So shall my word be that goeth forth out my mouth: it shall not return unto me void, but it shall accomplish that which I please, and it shall prosper in the thing whereto I sent it."* NOTE: God's Word on healing will accomplish healing in you.

Jeremiah 1:12 *"Then said the LORD unto me, Thou hast well seen: for I will hasten my word to perform it."* NOTE: God is looking, searching eagerly for someone to take Him at His Word so that He can perform it on their behalf.

Joshua 21:45 *"There faileth not aught of any good thing which the LORD had spoken unto the house of Israel; all came to pass."* NOTE: Whatever God has spoken in His Word, all comes to pass. His Word stands alone. His Word never fails.

Every good and perfect gift comes from above. Healing is a good gift from God! God has already destroyed the works of darkness and His gift of life, healing and health even as your soul prospers is yours.

James 1:17 *"Every good gift and every perfect gift is from above and cometh down from the Father of lights, with whom is no variableness neither shadow of turning."* Healing is a wonderful gift from God, and here again is another proof that He does not change. What He did yesterday He will do again today and forever. Praise the Lord, He is still the Healer!

1 Corinthians 3:21-22 *"Therefore let no man glory in men. For all things are yours. Whether Paul, or Apollos or Cephas, or the world, or life, or death, or* *things present, or things to come; all are yours."* NOTE: This says it so clear; the Lord is holding nothing back from us. Surely healing is included in the claim of 'all things' and certainly is included in the word "life." Begin to praise the Lord for your healing which is a gift to you from the Lord and the manifestation that will come as you receive the promise by faith.

Romans 11:29 *"For the gifts and calling of God are without repentance."* Note: He is the giver of gifts and He does not take them back, they cannot be canceled out!

Philippians 2:13 *"For it is God which worketh in you both and to do his good pleasure."*

Matthew 11:28 *"Come to me, all you who labor and are heavy-laden and overburden and I will cause you to rest {I will ease and relieve and refresh your souls}."* NOTE: "Rest" means to cease from toil or labor in order to recover and collect His strength, and implies a feeling of wholeness and well-being. Place your focus off of the circumstances, and begin praising Him for all that He has done for you. You are highly favored by God.

Galatians 3:13-14 *"Christ hath redeemed us from the curse of the law, being made a curse for us: for it is written, Cursed is every one that hangeth on a tree: That the blessing of Abraham might come on the Gentiles through Jesus Christ; that we might receive the promise of the Spirit through faith."* NOTE: The curse of the law includes sickness and disease and is found in Deuteronomy 28:15-68. But by the shed Blood of Jesus Christ we were purchased out of or out from under the curse.

Proverbs 26:2 *"As the bird by wandering, as the swallow by flying, so the curse causeless shall not come."* NOTE: As we continue in Christ, the curse has no right to take root in our lives. Take a firm stand against it, and command its effects to leave in the Name of Jesus! You are a child of the King.

Colossians 1:13 *"Who hath delivered us from the power of darkness, and hath translated us into the kingdom of his dear Son."* NOTE: Remember there is no sickness or disease in the Kingdom to God!

1 John 3:8b *"For this purpose the Son of God was manifested, that he might destroy the works of the devil."* NOTE: The reason the Son of God was made manifested (visible) was to undo, destroy, loosen and dissolve the works of the devil (has done). There is no doubt that sickness and disease are works of the devil, introduced to mankind through the fall as part of the curse. Jesus came to undo the works of the devil. Sickness and disease have no right to remain in your body as a child of God.

2 Corinthians 3:17 *"Now the Lord is the Spirit; and where the Spirit of the Lord is, there is liberty."* NOTE: The Spirit of God dwells within your heart. Freedom and Liberty from bondage in any form belong to you, and you should expect it. It is your covenant right!

John 8:36 *"Therefore if the Son makes you free, you should be free indeed."* NOTE: Not just free, but really unquestionably free. So if the son liberates you [makes you a free man], then you are really and unquestionably free.

Hebrews 12:12-13 *"Wherefore lift up the hands which hang down, and the feeble knees; And make straight paths for your feet, lest that which is lame be turned out of the way; but let it rather be healed."* NOTE: Real faith rejoices at the promises of God as if it were experiencing them already. Get the focus off of your problem and on the answer which are the promises of God—His Word!

Psalm 42:11 *"Why art thou cast down, O my soul? And why art thou disquieted within me" Hope thou in God: for I shall yet praise him, who is the health of my countenance, and my God."*

We have confidence in Him, for God cannot lie. Hold fast to your healing!

Hebrews 10:23 *"Let us hold fast the profession of our faith without wavering; [for he is faithful that promised]."*

1 John 5:14-15 *"And this is the confidence that we have in Him, that, if we ask any thing according to his will, he heareth us: And if we know that he hear us, whatsoever we ask, we know that we have the petitions that we desire of Him."* The Word of God is the will of God. Jeremiah 1:12 says that He watches over His Word to perform it. So when you ask and believe the Word of God, you are asking and believing according to His will and you receive, just as it says!

Hebrews 10:35-36 *"Therefore do not cast away your confidence, which has great reward. For you have need of endurance, so that after you have done the will of God, you may receive the promise."* NOTE: Remember that the will of God is the Word of God!

Long life belongs to you—do not give up! Base your faith on the promises of God! He promised you long life! See your healed self with your spiritual eye – next year, in the next five years and even in the next ten years!

Genesis 6:3 *"And the LORD said, My Spirit shall not strive with man forever, for he is indeed flesh; yet his days shall be one hundred and twenty years."* NOTE: The promise of God is that you live a good long life, even to 120 if you so desire! Speak to that mountain of death and command it to be removed. Begin to grab hold of this promise of long life and lay claim to it with your spoken words. Do not settle for less than what God has promised, do not let the devil steal from you. Go on and live a long life fulfilling your days, calling and ministry upon this Earth!

Psalm 90:10 *"The days of our years are threescore years and ten; and if by reason of strength they be fourscore years, yet is their strength labour and sorrow; for it is soon cut off, and we fly away."* This Psalm was written by Moses and this verse pertains to the disobedient children of Israel that came out of Egypt being led by Moses who, because of their unbelief, were condemned to live out their lives wondering in the desert until each one had died. Only their children and Joshua and Caleb would enter into the Promised Land. Moses went on to live 120 years and Scripture [Deuteronomy 34:7] says that his strength had not departed him and his eyes were not dim.

Job 5:26a *"Thou shalt come to thy grave in a full age..."*

Psalm 91:16 *"With long life will I satisfy him, and shew him my salvation."* NOTE: God is saying live until you are satisfied.

Psalm 118:17 *"I shall not die but live, and declare the works of the Lord."* NOTE: Agree with this right now! Declare it with your voice! God has a plan for my life here on Earth. Do not let the enemy steal it away. You can do what God says you can do, you can be what God says you can be!

CAST DOWN THOSE THOUGHTS AND IMAGINATIONS THAT DO NOT LINE UP WITH THE WORD OF GOD! STAY FOCUS ON WHAT THE WORD SAYS!

2 Corinthians 10:4-5 *"For the weapons of our warfare are not carnal, but mighty through God to the pulling down of strong holds; Casting down imagi-*

nations, and every high thing that exalteth itself against the knowledge of God, and bringing into captivity every thought to the obedience of Christ." NOTE: Keep your focus on the promises of God; you have to make yourself stay focused. Do not allow your mind to stray—the manifestation [the glory] of your healing is on its way!

STATE YOUR CASE TO GOD

Isaiah 43:25-26 *"I, even I, am he who blots out your transgressions for My own sake, and I will not remember your sins. Put Me in remembrance; let us contend together; state your case, that you may be justified [acquitted]."* NOTE: Your case was settled when Jesus went to the Cross on your behalf.

Your words are important, make sure you are speaking words of life – speaking healing, speaking wholeness, and speak good health!

Isaiah 57:19 *"I create the fruit of the lips..."* NOTE: The word "fruit" means produce. God creates what you produce from your mouth when we believe and speak with the Word of God.

Mark 11:22-23 *"For verily I say unto you, That whosoever shall say unto this mountain, Be thou removed, and be thou cast into the sea; and shall not doubt in his heart, but shall believe that those things which he said shall come to pass, he shall have whatsoever he saith. Therefore I say unto you, What things soever ye desire, when you pray, believe that ye receive them, and ye shall have them."* NOTE: What kind of mountains or obstacles do you have in your life right now? Obey Jesus and command that mountain of pain, cancer, disease to go NOW out of your body in the Name of Jesus. Jesus said you can have what you say. Begin to call your body whole, healed, well—do not stop, do not listen to your body, do not listen to doubt and fear, listen to Jesus, listen to His Word.

Job 22:26 *"Thou shalt also decree a thing, and it shall be established unto thee: and the light shall shine upon thy ways."*—Give voice to the promises in the Word, and lay claim to them as your inheritance. Decree that you are healed! Say out loud: **"Lord, you said that by your stripes I am healed, so on the authority of your Word, I decree that I am healed and that sickness and disease have no hold on me and they must go in the Name of Jesus!"**

We are already healed, justified (acquitted, made righteous) because of the blood of Jesus; God's Word never fails but accomplishes its purpose and therefore we win!

Acts 5:16 *"There came also a multitude out of the cities round about unto Jerusalem, bringing sick folks, and them which were vexed with unclean spirits: and they were healed everyone."*—All were healed. Jesus is the same yesterday, today and forever.

Hebrews 7:25 *"Wherefore he is able also to save them to the uttermost that come unto God by him, seeing he ever liveth to make intercession for them."*— Saved to the uttermost (completely, perfectly, finally and for all the time and eternity). "Save" the Greek word is sozo (to heal, preserve, save, do well, and be (make) whole). It means deliverance in the present as well in the future or in eternity, physical as well as spiritual.

Acts 13:39 *"And by him all that believe are justified from all things..."*—Justified (declared righteous) from all things. Train yourself to translate the word "justified" as declared righteous. {Just-if-I'd never sinned} That is righteousness to be in right standing with God. As born-again Believers we have become the righteousness of God in Christ. Through His shed blood, we are redeemed and declared righteous from ALL things.

Romans 8:11 *"But the Spirit of him that raised up Jesus from the dead dwell in you, he that raised up Christ from the dead shall also quicken your mortal bodies by his Spirit that dwelleth in you."*—Allow the Lord to impart His life into you by placing faith in His Word. Begin to praise Him for this promise.

Isaiah 53:4-5 *"Surely he hath borne our griefs [sickness and disease], and carried our sorrows [pain]; yet we did esteem him stricken, smitten of God, and afflicted. But he was wounded for our transgressions, he was bruised for our iniquities; the chastisement of our peace was upon him; and with his stripes we were {past tense} healed."*

1 Peter 2:24b *"By whose stripes ye were [past tense] healed."*

2 Corinthians 4:10-11 *"Always bearing about in the body the dying of the Lord Jesus that the life also of Jesus might be made manifest in our body. For we which live are always delivered unto death for Jesus sake, that the life also of Jesus might be made manifest in our mortal flesh."*—This is bodily health!

Matthew 6:9-10 *"After this manner therefore pray ye: Our Father which art in heaven, Hallowed be thy name. Thy Kingdom come. Thy will be done in earth, as it is in heaven."* NOTE: Jesus always prays the will of God, and when He prays that the will of God be done here on earth just as it is in heaven. People in heaven are not sick, so we can clearly see its God's will that we be free from sickness and disease. Amen!!!

John 6:63 *"It is the Spirit who gives life; the flesh profits nothing. The words that I speak to you are spirit and they are life."* NOTE: God's Word is healing, it will bring health to your flesh (Proverbs 4:22). That's why it is important to continue to go over the healing scriptures daily, therefore building your faith in the area of healing, imparting the very life of God into your cells. Fill up on God's Word.

Jeremiah 1:12 *"... I am alert and active watching over my word to perform it."* NOTE: God is looking, searching eagerly for someone to take Him at His Word so that He can perform it on their behalf.

Joshua 21:45 *"Not a word failed of any good thing which the Lord had spoken to the house of Israel. All came to pass."* NOTE: How much more sure is this promise to us since our covenant with God is based upon the shed Blood of Jesus Christ.

Deuteronomy 11:21 *"That your days may be multiplied, and the days of your children, in the land which the LORD sware unto your fathers to give them, as the days of heaven upon the earth."* NOTE: If a Believer honors God and live according to the Word, He says "that his days maybe multiplied, and the days of your children. God's plan is that His children begin to experience the inheritance of the heavenly life while here on the earth.

Deuteronomy 7:15 *"And the Lord will take away from thee all sickness, and will not put none of the evil diseases of Egypt, which thou knowest, upon thee; but will lay them upon all them that hate thee."* NOTE: We are under the New Covenant which is based upon the precious Blood of Jesus Christ.

Romans 8:32 *"He that spared not his own Son, but delivered him up for us all, how shall he not with him also freely give us all things."* NOTE: "Freely give us all things." Surely this includes healing!

Isaiah 40:31 *"But they that wait upon the LORD shall renew their strength; they shall mount up with wings as eagles; they shall run, and not be weary,* *and they shall walk, and not faint."* NOTE: The word "wait" implies a positive action of hope, based on knowing that the Word of God is a true fact and that it will soon come to pass—waiting with earnest expectation! Amen!

Psalm 34:19 *"Many of the afflictions of the righteous, but the LORD delivers him out of them all."*

Jeremiah 33:6 *"Behold, I will bring it health and cure, and I will cure them and will reveal unto them the abundance of peace and truth."*

Matthew 18:19 *"Again I say unto you, That if two of you shall agree on the earth as touching anything that they shall ask, it shall be done for them of my Father which is in heaven."* NOTE: The prayer of agreement is powerful— have someone agree with you for your healing.

Isaiah 58:8 *"Then shall thy light break forth as the morning, and thine health shall spring forth speedily..."*

Psalm 41:3 *"The LORD sustain, refresh, and strengthen him on his bed of languishing, all his bed you [O Lord] will turn, change and transform in his illness." (Amplified Version)* NOTE: "all his bed" in Hebrew meaning all that he is afflicted with, or all of his condition that he is lying with. It is always God's will to turn, change and transform our mourning into dancing.

1 Thessalonians 5:23 *"And the very God of peace sanctify you wholly; and I pray God your whole spirit and soul, and body be preserved blameless unto the coming of our LORD Jesus Christ."* NOTE: The word "blameless" means sound, complete and intact. Wholeness, wellness and health are for the complete make-up of man, spiritual, mental, and physical.

Psalm 103:2-3 *"Bless the LORD, O my soul, and forget not all his benefits: Who forgiveth all thine iniquities; who healeth all thy diseases."* NOTE: Healing is one of the benefits that belong to the Believer.

3 John 2 *"Beloved, I wish above all things that thou mayest prosper and be in health, even as thou soul prospereth."*

Jeremiah 17:14 *"Heal me O Lord, and I shall be healed; save me, and I shall be saved: for thou art my praise."* NOTE: Agree and say I have healing just as I have salvation, it is yours now!

James 5:14-15 *"Is any sick among you? Let him call for the elders of the church; and let them pray over him, anointing him with oil in the name of the LORD: And the prayer of faith shall save the sick, and the LORD shall raise him up; and if he have committed sins, they shall be forgiven him."* NOTE: Prayer of faith shall save the sick, and the LORD shall raise him up; and if he has committed sins, they shall be forgiven.

REMEMBER TO GIVE TESTIMONY OF YOUR HEALING!

Revelation 12:11 *"And they overcame him by the blood of the Lamb and by the word of their testimony..."* NOTE: When your healing manifests itself and you recover and have the opportunity to testify to the grace of the Lord—DO IT! The Lord wants you to give glory to Him for what He has done and it will also serve to help build faith in someone else who has a need.

HOLD ON TO YOUR HEALING

I cannot tell you when my body was completely made whole. All I know is one day...I noticed all the symptoms were gone! Praise God!!!!! The Spirit of the Lord revealed to me that I must hold on to my healing and He gave me this verse:

Nahum 1:7, 9b *"The Lord is good, a stronghold in the day of trouble; and He knows those who trust in Him...He will make an utter end of it. Affliction will not rise up a second time."* NOTE: After you receive the manifestation of your healing, this verse becomes your stand of faith.

Lord God,

I praise you for You are marvelous. I praise you for allowing me to encounter you as Jehovah Jireh and see your hand in my healing process. I worship you because You are God and there is none greater or mightier. Thank you for my healing and the healing of the one who has read my testimony. In Jesus name.

Amen.

And Finally

CONTINUE TO BELIEVE, SPEAK AND STAND ON GOD'S WORD

The Gospel that Jesus preached is the same gospel that I preach! The Bible is an owner's manual written to us by God, everything you need to know about our lives is in the Bible. I believe we can do what the Bible says we can do! It has changed my life forever and it is still changing my life. It brings forth great miracles.

<u>Remember; do not lose heart</u> if you do not get healed instantly. After prayer the power (Holy Spirit) of God will enter you and will continue to work in you. I have found that many people, who do not get an instant healing, make the mistake of going away and saying, 'I didn't get my healing.' This allows the devil to steal your healing miracle experience. Continue to BELIEVE God for your healing and your complete healing will follow. The provision for your healing is there.

Continue in your normal daily devotions and Bible reading, learning, growing and maturing irrespective of your situation. Continue to read Proverbs 4:20-22, Joshua 1:8. Also, begin to journal the little gems of truth the Lord reveals to you in your daily devotions. They will serve as an anchor to your soul as you refer back to them when the going gets tough.

When you finally come to the place when you are ready to make up your mind to receive your healing by faith, write down that date and settle it before the Lord in prayer. Not the date you want to see the manifestation take place in your flesh, but the day that you are going to put your faith to work to believe that He has already provided your healing. From that day forward you will no longer ask the Lord for healing, instead you will now thank Him and praise Him for it. This is where the battle begins as the enemy will attempt to talk you out of it in the days to come, trying to convince you that it didn't work or it's not for you. You may even hear him say, "oh sure, it worked for Robin McCray, but you're different, you're not like her, it won't work the same for you." *Do not you believe that lie*, the Bible tells us over and over that God shows no favoritism—He treats all His children the same—He is an equal opportunity God! You must stand strong in faith and must not give in. When the enemy says you are not going to get healed, you can now state with complete confidence and even have a little fun with it by saying, "Yes, you're right devil, I'm not going to receive my healing, because on this date devil, *I've already received my healing by faith*—you're just too late! It's mine now!!!"

Be careful not to put your healing in first place, we do not want it to become an idol. Keep the Lord and your relationship with Him and your love for Him in first place.

"And let us not grow weary while doing good (doing the Word), for in due season we shall reap if we do not lose heart." Galatians 6:9

Finally—Stand, and keep on standing! Dig your feet in and refuse to be moved from the truth of God's Word. Read Ephesians 6:10-18. **Do not waiver** because as it says in James 1:6-7, *"But let him ask in faith, nothing wavering. For he that wavereth is like a wave of the sea driven with the wind and tossed. For let not that man think that he shall receive any thing of the Lord."* **Never let go** of the promise. Know the difference between a miracle and a healing. Miracles are instant, and healings are progressive.

Meditate on the Word of God, focus in on them. Begin to see yourself in the light of the promises of God. See yourself as the Word says you are! The Lord paid an extremely high price for you to enjoy the benefit of them all. Do not speak your problem, but begin to speak the answer and watch your situations change!!!

God's Word is His will. Take it, it's yours!!!

A PRAYER OF DECLARATION:

Father, in the name of Jesus, I decree and declare over the person reading this book that they are healed, delivered and set free from all sickness and disease. According to your Word in Philippians 4:6-7, I speak peace to all anxiety, depression and chronic pain syndromes; all bipolar and schizo-affective disorders; all post-traumatic disorders, and I command their power to be broken from touching their life. I speak divine healing to their body in Jesus' name. I decree that he/she will draw near to You with a true heart in full assurance of faith, having their heart sprinkled from all evil conscience and their body washed in pure water. I decree and declare victory over the spirit of infirmities. I decree that they are healed of terminal cancer and tumors. You have already given then dominion and power over the enemy, and nothing shall by any means hurt them. I decree divine deliverance from every addiction in Jesus' name. They are healed and Spirit filled; sickness and disease is far from them. We give you praise in advance for what's already done! Amen.

About the Author

Prophetess Robin McCray has been active in church ministry for over twenty years. She carries a true pastor's heart, desiring to see the love of Christ consume and transform people lives. She is dedicated to empowering individuals to know who they are in God and that they have a destiny. God has called her forth as an apostolic voice to help produce and give birth to what the Spirit of the Lord is doing in the earth. She is a "forerunner" in the realm of the Spirit. As a forerunner, she is instructed to equip, strengthen and release the Body of Christ to fulfill their life purposes and prepare the way of the Lord.

God has placed upon her a cutting edge anointing that allows her message to come forth in freshness that penetrates deeply into the hearts of the hearers. She is known as a "ball of fire" when she speaks. Robin carries a strong prophetic mantle of God. She preaches under the anointing of the Word of God, which breaks through hard and impossible situations. The voice of this ministry speaks with great authority and the fire of the Holy Spirit that comes as a result of endless hours in intercession and in the presence of God Almighty.

The Spirit of the Lord is using Robin to speak at numerous churches and conferences releasing encouragement and healing to the Body of Christ. God has called her forth to be a Great Intercessor to go out of the four walls of the church into the world to disciple His people. She is called a midwife; that carries an anointing to help birth hidden treasures within individuals and elevate them to the next level of their destiny.

She is a part of, "Sisters on the Wall," an intercessory group birthed in March of 2007. She is the author of five books that's in the process of publishing," Restoring the Art of Intercession—The Watchmen Call, The Art of Waiting on God, The Power of True Worship, Unleashing the Power of the Mind and Medicine for the Body—The Word of God." She holds numerous awards, commendations and holds a B.S. of Business Degree from Barry University in Miami, FL.

Robin writes monthly newsletter through her blog: robinmccrayministries.blogspot.com

Robin has been married for over twenty-four years to her long life partner, Troy McCray and they are the parents of three children; Jasmine McCray, Troy McCray II and Jerami McCray

www.ingramcontent.com/pod-product-compliance
Lightning Source LLC
Chambersburg PA
CBHW062010040426
42447CB00010B/1993